D1742905

A Doctor's Search for Health

Hector W. Jordan

VANTAGE PRESS
New York

All biblical quotations are from
the King James Version of the Bible,
unless otherwise indicated.

Published by Vantage Press, Inc.
516 West 34th Street, New York, New York 10001

Manufactured in the United States of America
ISBN: 0-533-10529-3

Library of Congress Catalog Card No.: 92-94304

0 9 8 7 6 5 4 3 2 1

Contents

Preface

When I was about three years old I was very ill with broncho-pneumonia, and at one point my life was, I understand, despaired of. However, I recovered and from then on was considered a "delicate" child by my devoted parents. I was the youngest of eight and was the least strong, apart perhaps from a much loved sister, who died at the age of fifteen from leukaemia.

I suffered from most of the so-called children's ailments, so that when I reached my teens I began to wonder how I could get stronger. I believed firmly that God had created us and therefore intended us to be healthy in body and mind. God would not make mistakes, so the fault must somehow be ours, i.e., mankind's. Where had we gone wrong, either deliberately or ignorantly, or had we inherited the results of our forefathers' mistakes? Perhaps it was a combination of both.

From this time on I tried to improve my health in the only ways I knew how. I began to take physical exercise more seriously but lacked the staying power that other boys my age seemed to possess. However, I persevered with various forms of sport and gradually improved in health so that, by the time I left school for university, I considered myself reasonably fit, although I suffered two or three colds every winter and influenza about every third year. Fortunately, my constitution was sound and I had no physical or mental defects.

From an early age I was sure that I was meant to study medicine, and so I entered University College, in London, in October 1923. Here I was very fortunate in having some of the best teachers, and I enjoyed my time there and later in University College Hospital, where I learnt a great deal about disease but not much about health. I became fascinated with surgery and decided to specialise in ear, nose, and throat.

On the advice of Herbert Tilley, the senior surgeon at the Royal Ear Hospital, I joined a firm of doctors in Eastbourne in order to gain some experience of general practice before going on to concentrate on ENT surgery. In Eastbourne I met the Oxford Group, which had a profound effect on me and changed the course of my life.

In it I met my future wife, who was practising osteopathy and naturopathy (both rather frowned upon in the 1930s), and I became interested in what she was doing. I asked many questions and read some of her books; I eventually tried out these different methods of treatment on certain patients where all other treatments had failed. I was amazed at the results and became convinced that this was the right way since it got to the basic cause of disease and assisted the body's own healing resources to bring the patients back to health.

Eventually, and after much heart searching, I saw clearly that God's will for me was to follow this way and I gave up the idea of surgery, since I was hoping to educate people to become healthier and, therefore, avoid the need for surgery except in cases of trauma (injuries, etc.).

Over the years I have learned more and more about the whole man and the interrelationship of body, mind, and spirit, and in recent years I have felt the need for a book dealing with the health of man and society and environment—complete health. This book, therefore, is the result of gleanings from many sources and much pondering and experience for over fifty years. It is not a scientific treatise, although based on scientific facts, but is written for anyone and everyone in the hope that anyone reading it will gain something of practical value. There is a short bibliography for those who want to study this subject more fully.

I am deeply grateful to those who have gone before me, from whom I have learned about some aspects of health and healing. In particular, I am indebted to my wife, who started me on this quest and who has been my teacher and constructive critic—I owe a very great deal to her.

I am also indebted to Mrs. J. Larcombe and Mrs. C. Loadman and my good friend Richard Rumary, who all read the text and made valuable suggestions, and to Mr. W. A. Honey for having this manuscript typed and photocopied.

Introduction

Like everything around us, we are constantly changing. You are not the same person you were yesterday—not quite. Tomorrow you will be slightly different; you will be either slightly healthier and stronger or slightly weaker; you could be a slightly better person or slightly worse.

Our bodies are constantly changing because some cells die as they come to the end of their useful life and others join together and then redivide, forming new, rejuvenated cells. In this way we have a built-in system of repair and rejuvenation so that the body is always trying to heal itself, and it will do this if given the right conditions. Wounds will heal if kept clean and free from infection; fevers will resolve with rest and fasting. There is enough knowledge, unfortunately not yet widely known, about laws or conditions of health to enable the average person who follows them to reach a fairly high state of health.

Our minds also are constantly changing. We do not (or should not) think as we did ten, twenty, or thirty years ago. We are, or should be, acquiring knowledge and wisdom and gaining experience. Sadly, some people, especially as they grow old, cease to do much thinking and tend to stagnate.

There is a third part of us, the soul or spirit, and this follows the same basic laws that apply to the mind and body. Cultivate the life of the spirit and it will develop and grow; ignore it and it will atrophy.

Some people think of themselves as a body with a mind, others as a mind with a body. A few think of themselves as a spirit with a mind and a body. In fact, we are a trinity—a spirit, mind, and body—and the three are, during this life, completely inseparable and interdependent.

In consequence, there is interaction between all three, and in considering health we must think of total health—health of the whole person. The words *health, whole,* and *holy* come from the same Anglo-Saxon root and express a condition of complete health, a wholeness and holiness. On the other hand, each of these three parts of us lives, in a sense, on a different plane, and it is, therefore, easier to consider each one separately and then attempt a synthesis.

There is another point we must consider. We cannot separate ourselves from our surroundings, and these include not only the inanimate things around us, but also the other human beings and animals with which we come in contact. An individual is, willy-nilly, part of a community and is affected by it and also has an effect upon it. We act and interact upon each other—for good or ill. This means that the individual can only attain perfect health or wholeness when the whole community attains perfect health.

It follows that the more individuals in a society who approach health and holiness, the easier it becomes for each to reach the goal. Here we must emphasise that health is not something we can acquire like a new dress or suit; it is a continuous process, a continual becoming. We shall not attain it in this life, but we can make considerable progress provided we continue to advance. It is easy to slip back if we are not advancing—we cannot stand still. Moreover, the further we advance in health and holiness, the more we shall help those we are in contact with by acting as catalysts, inspiring them to join in the search for health and holiness.

Our surroundings (*environment* is the "in" word) also consist of the soil and the plant life growing from it. Our life and our health depend upon the soil. All the elements that go to make up our bodies come from the soil and the air. If the atmosphere is polluted (containing poisonous gases) or unbalanced (containing too much carbon dioxide or too little oxygen), then our health is bound to be affected. If the soil is poisoned or unbalanced, it will be unhealthy and cannot produce really healthy plants. Hence the animals, including man, that feed upon this plant life cannot be really healthy. We shall explore this more fully in a later chapter.

In the first two verses of chapter 12 of his letter to the Romans, Paul urges us to present our bodies as a living sacrifice, to have our minds renewed, and to be so transformed in nature as to be able to make out what is the Will of God. In modern terms, he is urging us to give ourselves—body, mind, and spirit—to the Lord. In order to give Him the best we can offer, we should strive towards total health.

I hope that this book will help some to do just that.

One / The Physical Body

We inherit our bodies from our parents and have to do the best we can with what we are given. Whether we inherit a good constitution or a bad one, we can do a great deal to improve matters, and even with a poor start, a much higher standard of health can be achieved by following a few simple rules:

1. *Correct Food:* The tendency until recently in "civilised" society has been to move away from natural foods towards refined and convenience ones; these are largely deficient in fibre, vitamins, mineral salts, and that intangible something that is present in fresh food (especially fruits and vegetables) and is not present in stale, refined, and chemically altered foods.
2. *Exercise:* Our bodies are machines—wonderful, amazingly intricate machines. Machines must be used or they deteriorate. Our bodies are no exception; in fact, the more they are used (within reason) the better they function. Exercise is necessary for physical health.
3. *Rest and Relaxation:* These are necessary so that everyday wear and tear can be repaired. The body has its own repair workshop and, given the chance, can do remarkable things in the way of repair.
4. *Care of the Skin:* The skin is a self-repairing, protective covering but is also an important organ. Its health depends largely upon the health of the whole body.

5. *Fresh Air:* At least some part of each day should, whenever possible, be spent outdoors. This is one reason why gardening is such good exercise. However well ventilated a building may be, it always contains more carbon dioxide and less oxygen than the open air. Most forms of central heating raise the temperature of the air within the house, which, of course, becomes stale (containing less oxygen), especially in cold weather, when windows and doors are kept closed. The healthiest form of central heating is one that heats air from outside and pumps it into the house, thus providing a supply of fresh, warmed air. There are many gaseous pollutants that damage the atmosphere, e.g., car exhaust fumes, domestic and factory chimney emissions, tobacco smoke, etc. These are all potentially dangerous to our lungs if inhaled in more than minimal amounts. The danger to health of tobacco should be well known by now. In some areas certain forms of radiation can be harmful, but on the whole, tobacco is much more injurious.

Correct Food

During the end of the last century and the beginning of this one, a movement came into being that emphasised what became known as Nature Cure. Its philosophy was that the body and mind of man contained within them forces of healing that always strive toward health and that most drugs are actually harmful. The followers of this movement spoke of food reform, maintaining that our diet had strayed so far away from natural foods that the food eaten by the great majority of us led to ill health. The reformers taught that we should adopt a natural diet, cutting out all refined and "unnatural" foods. Our diet should consist of whole-meal bread, whole cereals (brown rice, shredded wheat, oatmeal, etc.), plenty of vegetables (not pressure-cooked), fruit of various kinds (raw and cooked), salads (at least once daily), milk, butter (not margarine, which is produced by chemical processing), cheese, and nuts. Elaborate dishes are unnecessary and the person who adopts a simple diet like this finds that he appreciates mild and subtle flavours.

Salt is harmful, except if one uses a small amount in cooking. Adding salt to one's food creates an imbalance of minerals by supplying far too much sodium. The body needs other elements (potassium, calcium, iron, etc.), and too much sodium does great harm by upsetting the balance. Nature provides all the mineral salts we need if we eat plenty of vegetables, salads, and fruits.

Meat is best taken in small amounts or avoided altogether. Fish is the healthiest form of animal protein, but even that is in danger of being polluted by the effluents we pour into our rivers and the sea around our coastlines.

Refined foods particularly to be avoided are white flour and white sugar. Modern orthodox research and thinking holds that lack of fibre in the diet could be at least in part the cause of certain gastrointestinal troubles, heart disease, arteriosclerosis (hardening of the arteries), and diabetes. Real whole-meal (not just brown) bread, of course, contains the fibre, but it also contains other things lacking in white flour. White sugar has also been condemned in recent years.

Strong stimulants such as coffee, tea, and alcohol are also harmful. Weak tea and weak coffee do not do much harm.

All of these things the food reformers have been teaching for eighty years or more, and these views are at last being accepted by increasing numbers of the medical profession.

In the early part of this century Sir Robert McCarrison, a

doctor working in the then Indian Medical Service, noticed two things: first, that the various races in the subcontinent lived on widely different diets from those of Europeans and second, that the different races tended to develop different types of illnesses.

In particular, McCarrison noticed that the races of northern India, such as the Sikhs, Pathans, Hunzas, and Mahrattas, were of strikingly superiour physique to those of the rest of the subcontinent. The Sikhs, in particular, were of excellent physique and generally enjoyed very good health. Their food consisted of *chapattis* made from whole-wheat flour, milk and its products (clarified butter, buttermilk, and curds), pulses (sprouted Bengal *gram*), and plenty of raw fresh vegetables, such as carrot and cabbage, and fruits. Meat was eaten sparingly, about once a week. Of these peoples, Sir Robert McCarrison wrote: "They are the finest races of India, so far as physique is concerned, and amongst the finest races of mankind." McCarrison also pointed out that the Sikh diet should be adopted in its entirety if good health was desired. He found that when times were hard the poorer Sikhs would cut down on or even cut out milk and milk products and fresh vegetables. In these cases they often developed stones in the kidney or bladder. This never occurred in those on the full Sikh diet.

McCarrison condemns white flour as being deficient in important nutrients and points out that rice is a relatively poor cereal compared with wheat. Since rice is the staple diet of the average Bengali or Madrassi, his intake of protein is very low (by religion he is often a non-meat eater), and fresh vegetables and fruits are eaten sparingly, we have not far to look for the cause of the poor physique that in general characterises these people.

One of McCarrison's experiments was particularly instructive. He took two groups of rats, twenty in each, housed in large cages of the same dimensions:

One group was fed on a diet similar to that used by the Sikhs; the other on a diet such as is commonly used [pre-World War I] by the poorer classes in England. The latter diet consisted of white bread, margarine, oversweetened tea with a little milk (of which the rats consumed large quantities), boiled cabbage and boiled potatoes, tinned meats, and tinned jams of the cheapest sorts.

The first thing McCarrison noticed, as this experiment progressed, was that the members of the former, and well-fed, group lived happily together. They increased in weight and flourished. The other group did not increase in weight; their growth was stunted; they were badly proportioned; their coats were mangy and lacking in gloss; they were nervous and apt to bite the attendants; they lived unhappily together, and by the sixtieth day of the experiment they began to kill and eat the younger ones amongst them.

At the end of 187 days (corresponding to about 16 years in man), the survivors in both groups were killed and examined postmortem. Disease of the lungs was much commoner and gastrointestinal disease was frequent in the group fed on the poorer English diet, whilst the group on the Sikh diet was free from it.

Since the last war, research in various countries has corroborated parts or all of McCarrison's findings—the importance of vitamins and mineral salts and the need for roughage or fibre, all of which are taken care in the Sikh diet. One cannot say, of course, that the modern Sikhs (especially those living in large towns or away from their homeland) keep to the same diet that their fathers and grandfathers did at the beginning of the century.

One thing is certain, however, that if one wishes to have good physical health it is very important to follow a regime based upon that of the traditional Sikh diet. This would involve avoidance of all refined cereals and sugars—only whole-meal flour and whole-wheat breakfast cereals, unpolished or brown rice, and brown sugar such as Demerara and Barbados sugar. (Glucose is out as well as sucrose, the usual white sugar.)

Milk, butter, and cheese are important sources of protein and fat; margarine is not a natural food—it is manufactured by a complicated process from oils or fats derived from animals, including fish, and vegetables and also contains flavourings, colouring, and manufactured vitamins.

Pulses (peas, beans, etc.) provide a useful extra source of protein, vitamins, and mineral salts. The increasing fashion of eating sprouting pulses and grains is a good way of providing extra vitamin C.

Fresh vegetables and fruits are very important dietary constituents and should be eaten daily. McCarrison suggested to a friend that the very fresh "living" vegetable contained some extra health-giving substance that so far we have not been able to analyse. There is no doubt that very fresh vegetables and fruits have a much better taste than when kept for a while, so the fresher one's fruits, salads, and vegetables, the better.

This makes an excellent and varied diet, and all those who have tried it have found a noticeable improvement in health, sometimes a considerable improvement. Meat can be added but is not essential and, in any case, should be taken sparingly. It is interesting that recent research has shown that the bones of elderly vegetarians are stronger and less liable to fracture than those of nonvegetarians.

The work of MacKarnass has shown that allergies can result from overindulgence in certain foods and especially beverages. These allergies often produce mental symptoms that will disappear when the offending item of diet is discovered and eliminated.

Of various food additives, the most common is ordinary salt—sodium chloride. Now the body needs sodium and chlorine, but it also needs potassium, calcium, and iron and traces of other elements, such as iodine, sulphur, etc. When sodium chloride is taken with food one can be taking 50 to 500 times as much as the body requires, and this puts a strain on the kidneys, which have to eliminate the excess. It also upsets the balance between the elements because the kidneys, in eliminating the sodium, will also be filtering out the calcium, potassium, etc., so that there will be a shortage of these elements. These elements are provided in natural foodstuffs in sufficient quantity and in balanced amounts for the use of the physical body. There are many other substances that are added to foods, and these are best avoided, especially sodium glutamate (of which the Chinese are especially fond).

Of recent work on the relation of diet to health, the one that caught my eye was a report in Moscow's *Literary Gazette* by a woman doctor, Galina Shatalova, in which she describes surprising results when patients with diabetes, asthma, and allergic troubles are put on to "natural" diets. She claims that her patients not only improve physically, but also lose their irritability and become happy, contented, and kind. I think she must have read McCarrison! She is against eating meat more than once a week and says that she tries not to kill biologically active substances. Vegetables should, therefore, be eaten raw or very lightly boiled.

I believe that alcoholic drinks are best avoided. Alcohol is a poison, and a sufficient quantity taken in a short time can kill. Even in small amounts, when taken over a long period of time it undoubtedly has a harmful effect on the body and mind. Recent research has shown that quite small doses will cause a temporary rise in blood pressure. In my opinion alcohol is best kept for medicinal purposes only. In certain cases regular use leads to addiction, and it is tragic to see the effect addiction has on the body, mind, and spirit of the person thus afflicted, and not only on the addict himself, but on his family and close friends. Having seen so much devastation caused by alcohol, I never advise it as a drink and therefore never touch it myself.

To sum up, one should avoid all very refined and processed foods. Food should be in as natural a state as possible, and ideally some raw food should be eaten at every meal.

Research done in Vienna between the wars strongly suggested that all cooking results in the formation of toxic substances. These could be counteracted or inhibited by eating some raw food, but, when the food is pressure-cooked no amount of raw food can prevent the formation of these toxic substances. Now almost all tinned foods are pressure-cooked, so it is best to avoid tinned foods or use minimal amounts only in emergency.

For much the same reason natural, unpasteurised milk is definitely superiour to pasteurised or sterilised milk. Heating milk destroys the beneficial bacteria, and the milk in this country (apart from the extremely rare exception) is free of the germs of tuberculosis and brucellosis (glandular fever), so that pasteurisation should be unnecessary.

Last, it is important not to overeat. Actually, most people find this form of diet very satisfying and there is a strong tendency to stop when one has had sufficient food.

Exercise

Any machine that is not used—not exercised—will deteriorate, and this applies to living machines as well as man-made ones. The body must be used if it is to remain healthy. The person who sits most of the day will either get overweight or develop coronary disease.

Our bodies have one great advantage over man-made machines—they repair themselves; in fact, they are continually repairing themselves, and the more well exercised they are the better the repair process is. The form of exercise we adopt is not important, provided the whole body is involved. And it does not have to be very strenuous; in fact, a daily walk is sufficient, although games of various kinds are good, as they bring variety. Many systems of exercise have been evolved and have achieved popularity for a time but are not necessarily any better healthwise than walking, swimming, or gardening. The important thing is that exercise should be regular and not too strenuous for the age of the participant.

Rest and Relaxation

It is during periods of rest and sleep that repair of the wear and tear of everyday use takes place. Our tissues and organs are regenerated and our whole body refreshed. Different people need different amounts of sleep, but in general, people who adopt a diet as outlined above need less sleep than those eating the usual refined and processed foods. Young people seem to need more sleep, possibly because they are generally more active.

Sleep is more beneficial if the sleeper is relaxed, and it is important to learn how to relax so that one does not begin the night in a tense state. Many books have been written on relaxation and many methods described, but I have found very few of these satisfactory, as they are mostly far too complicated.

Here is a very simple and effective system: Lie down and get as comfortable as possible. Have a good stretch. Think about your breathing, which should not be altered from normal; as you breathe out, imagine that you are breathing out some of your tension. As you do this, with each expiration you will find yourself getting more relaxed as time goes on. If you do this for twenty minutes each day and again at bedtime, you will find by the end of a month that you are much less tense and are able to keep calmer in moments of crisis.

Exercise and rest should go hand in hand. A good example of this is the heart. The heart muscle works continuously, but in between each beat it has a period of rest when the muscle relaxes completely before the next beat. In this way the heart can go on working for perhaps 70, 80, or even 100 years!

Care of the Skin

The skin is a remarkable living, waterproof covering for our bodies that is more than just a protective jacket. Primitive man living in cold localities grew a thick covering of hair to keep himself warm. Over the centuries, the wearing of clothing has suppressed the growth of the body hair, which is no longer required. Hair is not the only insulation against cold; immediately beneath the epidermis, or outer skin, is a layer of fatty tissue that varies in thickness in different individuals and is usually thicker in women.

The skin also contains, in its deepest layers, muscle fibres that in cold weather contract, causing a puckering of the skin (gooseflesh) and making the hairs stand on end. Both these effects tend to slow down heat loss, and when our early forebears had more hair the insulation was even better.

Not only can the skin slow down heat loss, but it can have the opposite effect in hot weather. This is done mainly by sweating, the evaporation of the watery sweat having a cooling effect. Sweat glands are very numerous, especially in certain areas of the body, such as the armpits. In normal health a fair amount of imperceptible sweating takes place—anything up to a quart in twenty-four hours. In fact, the sweat glands to some extent complement the kidneys in removing soluble waste products from the body. Apart from the sweat glands we also have in our skins sebaceous glands, which secrete an oily substance that lubricates the skin and helps to keep it healthy.

It is important that we look after our skin. Although a quick, hot bath for cleansing purposes is not harmful, a long soak in hot water is not good (except for medicinal purposes) and should be followed by a cold shower. The Finns follow their spell in the sauna by throwing pails of cold water over each other or rolling in the snow!

The choice of soap is important; a superfatted soap is best, such as a good Castile or a soap made from seaweed or plant ash. Overuse of talc powder can clog the pores.

Although exposure to the sun is beneficial in small doses, long exposure can be harmful and, in some cases, lead to skin cancer.

Clothing should always be as light as possible, i.e., just sufficient for warmth, and not tight-fitting so as to allow the skin to "breathe" and for free movement of the body.

Fresh Air

There is really nothing to add to what I said on this subject at the beginning of this chapter, except to stress its great importance. When you are outdoors, especially in the country, a few deep breaths from time to time are very beneficial. By burning up so much fossil fuel (coal, gas, oil, etc.), we pollute the atmosphere with increasing quantities of carbon dioxide, carbon monoxide, sulphur dioxide, and nitrogen dioxide. This is why it is wise for town dwellers to get into the country from time to time. Oxygen is essential for life and health, but too much oxygen is very harmful and can lead to brain damage. The atmosphere contains the correct proportion—twenty percent.

Two / The Mind

In the case of the body we have the advantage of being able to see it and dissect it, examine it, and x-ray it; we can look at its tissues and organs under the microscope. We can thus understand its anatomy, i.e., its structure. And what a marvellous structure it is! The Psalmist says we are fearfully and wonderfully made, and I cannot think of a better description. In the study of human physiology we learn of the workings of the body, this amazing machine that can go on working for seventy years or longer, which is infinitely more complicated than any man-made machine and has its own built-in repair system.

When we come to study the mind, we cannot even see it or feel it. And the only tool we have for examining the mind is the mind itself; it is like a computer trying to understand itself and how it works. In spite of these problems, we do understand, or think we do, a great deal about the mind and its workings. It was, in particular, Freud and Jung who showed us the way to begin to understand the mind by probing into its deeper layers and thus gaining insight into the way it works.

To begin with, we must not think of the mind as something static. It is better to think of it in terms of the "stream of consciousness" during which thoughts follow one after another. A useful simile is that of a river. The upper few inches of water would represent our conscious mind; this is where messages from the outside world come in through our sense organs—eyes, ears, skin, etc.—and are analysed and responded to. Conscious decisions are made here and actions

12

determined and carried out. Below the upper layer, the next layer—probably considerably deeper than the conscious layer—is the subconscious mind; this is where a large part of the memory is stored. The subconscious goes on working even during sleep and is the originator of dreams. Its reactions are much swifter than those of the conscious mind and enable us to act instantaneously (instinctively) in an emergency. If a child or animal darts out into the road in our path, we do not think, *there's a child—I must brake;* before we have time to think consciously our foot has stamped on the brake pedal. The subconscious mind has bypassed the conscious mind in a flash. Below the subconscious stream is the unconscious mind, that part that regulates bodily functions such as heart rate, temperature regulation, digestion, etc. As its functions are almost entirely automatic, we can for the time being disregard it. It works mainly through the hindbrain.

Like the body, the mind must be used if it is to develop. It needs exercise, but that exercise can be good or bad—we can think good thoughts or evil thoughts. To think good thoughts we need to think positively, to see the best in everything, including people, to think lovingly and constructively, and, above all, to be thankful for all the good things in life. The person who thinks good thoughts is likely to do good things—the opposite applies to the person who thinks evil thoughts.

The mind needs good food, and there is plenty of this to be had—good books, good music and other forms of good art, good conversation—the list is long. There is also plenty of bad food—bad books, bad plays, bad conversation, etc.—and if we are seeking good mental health we should avoid these.

I believe that appreciation of beauty is important for mental health, and beauty can be found everywhere if we only look for it. The beauty of the countryside is of course obvious both in the broad vistas but also in the individual organisms—trees, shrubs, flowers, insects, birds, etc. Look at the parts of these organisms—the bird's feather, the leaf, the pinecone—all things of beauty in their individual way. Look even closer—examine the leaf or the feather microscopically and see the incredible structure of the cells. Even in the busiest town there is beauty, much of it man-made, and this can and should be appreciated. There are beautiful children, beautiful women, and beautiful men. We should appreciate all these and thank God.

It would seem that the subconscious mind never forgets. Memories stored can be brought to light under hypnosis. Often dreams help in uncovering "hidden" memories. Sometimes an incident is so painful, either physically or mentally, that we determine to forget it. But the subconscious does not forget, and sometimes during sleep, when repression is relaxed, an incident we tried to forget is relived, and this may produce a nightmare or something like it.

To give an example, a friend of mine once said, "I can only stay with relatives or near friends because of the screaming."

"What do you mean by the scream?" I asked.

She replied, "I wake every night at 2:00 A.M. screaming—then I go to sleep again."

"You were dreaming," I answered.

"I never dream."

"You do but don't remember your dreams. Now tonight when you wake, try hard to remember what you were dreaming about."

She did this, and the next morning she rang up and said, "You were right. I was dreaming. It was a horrible muddle—all nuts and bolts."

"Good," I said. "Now tonight try again to remember."

She rang up again the next morning. "It was horrible—a train was crossing a bridge, and the whole thing collapsed into the river. And, do you know, I didn't scream so loudly?"

14

I said, "Do you think it was to do with the Forth Bridge disaster, when this actually happened?"

She thought for a little and then agreed that it was; she was a girl at the time of the accident, and it had had a considerable effect upon her impressionable mind. She never woke again and screamed in the night.

This story demonstrates the importance of never trying to forget sad or painful incidents; these should be faced squarely and honestly and seen in perspective as incidents that have to be lived through in the whole life span. Every experience in life can be used for good, but if repressed it can become a canker. Saint Peter in his first letter says: "At present you are temporarily harassed by all kinds of trials and temptations. This is no accident—it happens to prove your faith, which is infinitely more valuable than gold, and gold . . . must be purified by fire" (J. B. Phillips trans.).

There is no doubt that there are powers of the subconscious mind that are rarely, if ever, used. We are only beginning to understand some of its capabilities. Such things as telepathy, dowsing or water divining, premonitions and premonitory dreams, levitation, and many other things need further careful investigation. Perhaps one day we shall learn how to control these capabilities. We can certainly use our subconscious with a little training. When we have a problem we cannot solve, we sometimes say, "I'll sleep on it," and when we wake the solution is often there. We can also train the subconscious to wake us at a certain time.

Above all, we should keep our minds always alert and questioning. We can be alive to all that happens around us, or we can go to sleep mentally. It is a fact that many people go through life only partly awake, aware only of the thing immediately ahead, as if they have tunnel vision. More than once in his letters Saint Paul urged us to "Awake" or "Wake up." Make a habit of noticing things—the flight of a bird, the head of a lizard or a weasel popping out of the grass verge, trees blowing in the wind, the amazing variety of cloud patterns, the glory of the sunset.

Like the body, the mind is a very complicated machine, but also like the body, it can be healthy if certain simple rules are followed. These are the same as for the body. It needs healthy food, it needs regular exercise (i.e., it should be used as fully as possible), it needs rest and recreation, and it needs to be kept free of clutter—old hidden and painful memories that act like foreign bodies (often creating sepsis). These hidden memories can be evacuated by opening up the subconscious in much the same way as a doctor would lance an abscess. The process may be painful—and you may need professional help—but the relief is enormous.

Three / The Spirit

Physical life begins with the fusion of two cells, male and female. The female cell, or ovum, is a minute cell with enormous potential, but it achieves nothing of that potential until it is stimulated by the entry of the sperm cell, which then fuses with it. From then on the building of a body takes place and eventually a baby is born.

This baby is at first totally dependent upon his mother, but as he grows he becomes, in time, an independent being. He is, of course, endowed with a mind, which is at first very limited, but this mind has great potential and this potential will never be achieved without the impact of other minds upon it. On rare occasions human babies have been reared by animals of other species, and they tend to develop mentally like their foster parents and once "grown up" seem unable to become fully human. On the other hand, the child whose mind is stimulated by contact with "great" minds will usually attain a higher degree of intelligence than one raised in uninspiring surroundings. A challenge is needed if excellence is to be achieved.

Man is not only born with an undeveloped mind; he is also endowed with a potential spirit. Like the ovum, the potential spirit can only develop and grow if stimulated by a greater force than itself—the spirit of God. The human spirit can then grow and develop, but for this it needs food and exercise, the best possible. The potential spirit is able to resist the entrance of the Holy Spirit, and in this case it can only wither away. Does it then die, or can it be revived? But when the Holy Spirit is welcomed the effect can be revolutionary and the person is quite changed. And as he develops (Paul calls it "growing in grace") there comes a sense of confidence and inner peace that nothing can destroy.

But to grow an individual must take in the right food by reading and studying the Bible and other books that are both stimulating, challenging, and inspiring; he needs to breathe the right atmosphere of prayer and meditation, to learn to relax and rest in the love of God and to exercise his "spiritual gifts" by telling others of his experience of God's love and forgiveness. Above all, he needs the company of fellow believers, especially in giving thanks and worshipping the One Who created us and Who forgives us our deliberate sins and mistakes when we truly repent.

At some time in our lives we all need the healing of the spirit. If we want healing of the body we must turn away from the things that make us ill: the wrong food, lack of exercise, misuse of tobacco and alcohol and other drugs, etc., and adopt a healthy way of living. In the same way, if we desire healing of the spirit we must turn away from (repent) the things that harm our spiritual life, i.e., all evil influences such as bad books and films, bad company, bad thoughts and wrong practices, and turn to the Lord Christ, who is the one who through his spirit can invade our spirits and transform them.

The more completely we surrender our lives to Christ, the more fully does his life become ours. This brings what Paul calls, in Galatians 5, "the fruits of the spirit." These are, first, love, of which John says: "There is no fear in Love; but perfect love casteth out fear," and, "This commandment have we from Him, that he who loveth God love his brother also." And John, in his first letter, says: "We know that we have passed from death to life, because we love the brethren . . . Whosoever hateth his brother is a murderer: and no murderer hath eternal life abiding in him." This "eternal life" is the abundant life that

18

Jesus himself speaks of when he says, "I am come that they might have life, and have it more abundantly." Anyone who has experienced, even in a small measure, this abundant (eternal) life knows it is unmistakable—it is *life plus!* This is the true spiritual health.

The other fruits of the spirit are just manifestations of love. Joy is love rejoicing. Shortly before his crucifixion Jesus said, "These things have I spoken unto you, that my joy might remain in you, and that your joy might be full." Clearly he intends us to enjoy life to the full. We should be glad (rejoice) when things go well for others as well as ourselves. We can rejoice and give thanks for all the beauty we can see around us—beauty in nature, art, music, and architecture, the beauty of form and movement of man, woman, child, and animals.

Peace is love at rest. Jesus said, "Peace I leave with you, my peace I give unto you . . . Let not your heart be troubled, neither let it be afraid" (John 14:27). True inner peace is given to the one who has a deep love for God, and this is the antidote to fear.

Long-suffering is love suffering. In that glorious passage about love, 1 Corinthians 13, Paul says: "Love suffereth long." The ultimate expression of suffering love is in the Cross on which Our Lord showed the extent to which God would go in His love for us. Love will ultimately overcome suffering.

Gentleness is the expression of love. "Love is kind" (1 Cor. 13 once more). Gentleness is love in action; it is the result of loving.

Goodness is love in essence. There is no such thing as bad love. True love is essentially good and "rejoiceth not in iniquity, but rejoiceth in the truth" (1 Cor. 13).

Faith is love believing. Again Paul wrote in 1 Corinthians 13: "Love . . . believeth all things." And love trusts. When I was young my wife and I used to tell our children that "*faith* means forsaking all, I trust Him." It still seems to me a good definition.

Then there is meekness. True love is self-effacing. "Love . . . vaunteth not itself, is not puffed up" (1 Cor. 13).

Temperance (self-control) is love in control. If the spirit is directing my life, self-control follows, and "love . . . endureth all things" (1 Cor. 13).

All of these are symptoms of spiritual health. They are present in those who have been invaded by the spirit of God.

Four / The Environment

The environment affects us from the moment of birth onwards. The newborn baby is terribly vulnerable and is totally dependent upon his mother or mother substitute. His basic needs are love, security, and food. I put them in this order because I believe it is better for a child to be reared in an atmosphere of love and on the wrong food rather than on the healthiest diet possible and in an atmosphere of hate, which can affect that person for the rest of his life. But ideally a child should have all three.

Naturally, the best diet for a baby is that wonderful and perfect baby food, his own mother's milk. It is a perfectly balanced food, at the right temperature and completely germ-free. There is no real substitute, only approximations. Incidentally, the Hunza mother breast-feeds her child for two years, and the Hunzas are one of the healthiest races in the world. Probably the nearest to human milk is asses' milk, which is not easily obtainable in this country. Diluted cow's or goat's milk is next best, but usually powdered milk (not the best substitute) has to be resorted to when breast milk fails. It is best for the child to live mainly on milk for at least nine months.

I advise grape juice, rather than orange juice, which does not suit all babies, beginning with the juice of one grape at one month of age and increasing by one grape every four weeks. At about six weeks a little soft fruit—grape, pear, banana, etc.—can be added, and later whole cereals such as shredded wheat can be added. From nine to eighteen months the diet can be gradually built up to take the shape of the adult diet suggested earlier.

The baby that is loved by his parents and older brothers and sisters will feel secure. It is increasingly being realised that mother and baby should be in close proximity from the moment of birth. If mother or child is ill and needs special treatment, temporary separation may be necessary, but whenever possible they should be close together. Breast-feeding and handling of the baby help to build up a special relationship of love and trust that will continue as the child grows. Fathers also should handle their babies and do their share of bathing and nappy changing.

The baby that is brought up on a healthy diet and in a loving and secure environment, and in a praying household, is fortunate indeed and will almost certainly develop into a strong, healthy, and caring person.

Our environment includes, of course, other people—relatives, friends, and neighbours. We should strive to live at peace with all, as Paul admonished us. More than this, Our Lord told us to "love them" and this we must do, even though we may hate the things they do.

Animals are included in our environment, and it is important that our relationship with them is right. We should study and try to understand our domestic pets and treat them correctly. They have personalities of their own and deserve our respect. Cats are self-sufficient and tend to look upon their owners as equals or even inferiours. On the other hand, dogs are essentially pack animals and are happiest when they have a leader. A dog will look upon its master or mistress as its leader if it has been trained with firmness and love, just as one should train young children. A dog trained in this way from puppyhood will be obedient and will return the affection shown it. And how amazingly loyal a dog can be, and what wonderful friends they make! Animals reared correctly will always respond to kindness.

Cruelty to animals is sheer wickedness. There is a story told of Robert Louis Stevenson: One day he saw a man beating a donkey and told him to stop. "What's it to do with you?" said the man. "It's not your donkey." "No," replied Stevenson, "it's God's donkey, and I'm here to see you treat it properly." We must not forget that all animals belong to God and He expects us to treat them properly.

This leads to all kinds of questions—breeding animals for sport, experiments, food, etc. This is not the place to go into detail on these matters, but I believe we should all examine and question our attitude to these points. Jesus said that his Father was aware of the death of a sparrow. So He must be concerned about the death (and ill-treatment) of any of His creatures.

Plants are essential to our environment. We depend upon fruits, nuts, and vegetables for a large part of our sustenance. Grass and other vegetation feed the animals on which we depend for work, companionship, and, sadly, food.

Trees are essential to the health of the soil and the environment in general. When the farmers of the Midwest went in for wholesale tree felling the land dried out and the topsoil blew away, removing the fertile soil that had taken centuries to build up. Trees retain water in the soil, thus helping to prevent flooding; they add to the fertility of the soil by the annual leaf fall, which builds up a layer of compost on the surface. They also have a fascinating relationship with fungi, which is beautifully described by Dr. Louise Rayner in her book, *Trees and Toadstools.*

The Sahara was once forested. In fact, it is reckoned that all the world's deserts are man-made. Reclamation can take place and is happening in parts of the world by planting trees—it is a slow and tedious process, but it works. For sixty years or more Jews have been planting trees in what is now Israel, and they have truly made the desert "blossom like the rose."

When tree felling is done on a large scale in tropical countries the results can be devastating, bringing drought and consequent malnutrition and famine. Ethiopia is a case in point. The clearing of tropical rain forests (as in the Amazon basin) will have an even worse effect, which could alter weather patterns over a wide area of the world. The Men of the Trees have done valuable work in pointing out these terribly important functions of trees and tree cover, and their founder, Sir Richard St. Barbe Baker, was able to persuade countries like Algeria and Morocco to adopt policies of replanting the Sahara, beginning at the edge of the desert and moving south.

Before one fells any tree, very careful thought should be taken. A Swede once told me that in his country when they felled a tree they planted two in its place. Where there are too few trees, soil erosion will take place, as in parts of East Anglia in recent years where trees have been felled and hedges grubbed out. All those who have anything to do with the land should read *Silent Spring,* by Rachel Carson.

Grass is also an important part of the environment. A good covering of grass tends to prevent soil erosion, as one can see on hills such as the Downs, Exmoor, and Dartmoor. Grass also adds fertility to the soil by increasing its humus content. Moreover, old established grassland contains many herbs (which we call weeds when they appear on our lawns) that are valuable as food elements for grazing animals since they contain necessary trace elements.

The soil is, naturally, supremely important, since all our food resources ultimately derive from it. The soil is healthy when it has a high level of fertility; it will then produce healthy and abundant crops. This high level of fertility can be attained by returning all animal and vegetable waste to the soil, preferably after composting these together.

In the northern part of Kashmir is a tribe known as the Hunza, who live in a valley along which runs a river. Their fields are terraced on the lower slopes of the hills and irrigated by water from the river. The Hunza grow wheat, vegetables, and some fruits; they also keep cattle and their diet is very similar to that of the Sikhs as described in chapter 1.

The Hunza are remarkably fit and strong; they live longer than most Indian races and still play polo, their national game, well into their seventies. They carry loads of up to 120 pounds on their backs up and down the mountain passes and are eagerly sought as porters on mountain-climbing expeditions, etc. They are a cheerful and happy people and enjoy working. They are a perfect example of the natural wheel of life—a healthy soil growing healthy plants, which are eaten by animals and humans, whose excreta, together with unwanted plant material (e.g., straw, haulm of legumes, etc.), is returned to the soil to keep up its level of health. I have no doubt myself that food grown organically, i.e., without the use of chemical fertilizers but only with natural manure and compost, is much better and more health-giving. It is always worth paying a little more for "natural foods."

A very important part of our environment is of course the atmosphere. We cannot live without oxygen, and the amount in the air (about 20 percent) is the best amount for us, the remainder being mainly nitrogen and a small amount of carbon dioxide.

The problem is that we keep polluting the atmosphere in various ways; burning of fossil fuels produces some carbon monoxide, which is extremely poisonous—a fact well known, as so many commit suicide by using a car's exhaust. Owing to the heating of houses by oil, gas, and coal and the concentration of motor vehicles, the air in towns is much more polluted than that in sparsely populated areas. Certain factories create poisonous gases, which sometimes escape. The smoking of tobacco is harmful to both the smoker and others, especially in confined spaces; it has been clearly shown that tobacco has a part in the causation of various lung diseases, including bronchitis and cancer, certain forms of heart and arterial disease, and possibly some other disorders.

Water, together with air, is essential to life and health. Our bodies consist mainly of water, so it is important that we have access to a pure water supply. Unfortunately, the water in many large towns has been reprocessed several times and is, in a sense, "dead." It tastes flat and insipid. Water from a clear spring or a good well has an entirely different flavour—it is "living." If obtainable, this water is much better for health. It can be polluted so easily, by chemical waste from factories, by leakage of sewage or slurry, by chemicals (especially nitrogen compounds) washed from farmland into rivers. We need to be ever-vigilant.

Five / The Whole Person

We have been considering the three parts of the "whole man," i.e., the man who is truly healthy in body, mind, and spirit. Let us now see how these interact and work together to make the whole person.

There is no doubt that the three parts tend to operate on their own and on different levels. The body, for instance, being broadly three-dimensional, thinks almost entirely of the present; it is self-centred, engaged in working for its own survival, pleasure, and reproduction. The mind is largely four-dimensional, since it is aware of time. It cannot only think in the present; it can think of the past and of the future. In fact, some people spend a lot of time in the past (*living in the past* is a common expression) whilst others may spend a lot of time in the future (daydreaming). The spirit, however, belongs to a higher dimension, although it can operate in this space-time world. Paul describes how his spirit was "caught up into the seventh heaven," where he heard things he had never heard before.

Many people down the ages, many quite simple people, have had mystical experiences when they saw or heard things beyond this world. There are well-attested instances of people who, at the point of dying, saw into the "next world" and spoke of relatives and friends coming to meet them. We ourselves knew a dear old lady of ninety before the war who contracted pneumonia. We knew she would not get better, although she quite expected to. Then one day, in the presence of her two daughters, she began speaking to someone invisible to them;

after a pause she said to them, "Your father has just been to see me. He says that he and your sister are coming to fetch me quite soon. Isn't that lovely?" The next day she passed on peacefully into that fuller life.

I have read of a number of instances similar to this one, and the one that struck me most was of an American woman who was dying of cancer. She told her sister she wanted no painkillers, as she wished to be fully conscious at the point of death; when that moment came her face lit up and she exclaimed, "There's a wonderful light and lots of people coming towards me—Mother and Father and Ruth and Mary and . . . Olive, but why Olive? Oh, I understand." Olive was a close friend who had died in an accident about two weeks before. They had kept the news from her, thinking it could upset her and make her condition worse.

It does seem that certain individuals do sometimes have these mystical experiences and many people have had at least one—perhaps a voice or a vision. We are then privileged to glimpse that higher-dimensional world.

Try to imagine a two-dimensional world. It would have length and breadth, but no width or thickness. Imagine a pane of glass with no thickness, and you have a two-dimensional world. Now the only creature that could exist in such a world would be flat. Such a being could move freely in its two-dimensional habitat but could not move or see beyond it, i.e., into the three-dimensional world surrounding it and containing it. It would probably think, if it thought about such matters, that its two-dimensional world was the only form of existence. If I wished to communicate with the inhabitants of this world, I should have to become a flat being myself in order to enter their world and speak to them. Since it would be impossible for them to understand or visualise three-dimensional objects I would find it extremely difficult to tell them what our world is like; I could only give them a very small idea of what our life in this world is like by using picture language and similes—in fact, parables.

Now this may sound very silly and farfetched, but just add on one or two dimensions. We live in a three-dimensional world (or four-dimensional, if we include time as the fourth dimension). If there are worlds of higher dimensions (and currently many scientists think there are at least eleven dimensions), those worlds would be infinitely greater and more beautiful than this one in which we live. We would have no means of knowing anything about this larger world or worlds unless some being from that world appeared in this world in the form of a man.

But this is just what has happened! A man claimed to be the Son of God and to have come from God. He claimed to be the truth. Either he spoke the truth or he was mentally deranged or a charlatan. The person portrayed in the four Gospels could not possibly be either of the latter, so he must have been the Son of God, and it is imperative for us to listen to him. He told us that God loves us so much that He sent His Son to save us from our sins and from ourselves so that we could be free, free to live for God, free to love Him and to love our fellow beings. I wonder if we can fully grasp what a tremendous happening this is? In the words of J. B. Phillips, we are a "visited planet," and the visitor has come from a domain so enormously different—larger and more beautiful—from our four-dimensional world that it is quite impossible for us to begin to imagine what it is like.

Our Lord could only use human language (Aramaic) to speak of things beyond our comprehension. He spoke in parables—the Kingdom of Heaven is like a sower, a pearl of great price, a net thrown into the sea, etc. We, with our limited understanding, are apt to see one side of the truth and tend to think we have it all.

There is a very ancient story that can be found in the Hindu

Scriptures and also in one of the Islamic sacred writings. It differs somewhat in different forms, but the essential message is the same and clear: An elephant was put into a darkened room, and five men who had never seen an elephant were asked to feel it. Afterwards they were asked what the elephant was like. They each gave a different reply. One felt its trunk and said, "The elephant is like a snake"; the second felt its ear and said, "The elephant is like a fan"; the third felt its leg and said, "The elephant is like a tree"; the fourth felt its side and said, "The elephant is like a wall"; the fifth grasped its tail and said, "The elephant is like a piece of rope." And there was great dissention between them, because each one knew he was right. But the story goes on: if only someone had taken a lighted candle, they would have seen that none of them had got the whole truth, but each certainly had got a small part of it.

With our four-dimensional minds we cannot possibly grasp the whole truth, which is multidimensional. Paul said that we can only know in part, but we shall one day have full knowledge. So we have no right to feel superiour to our neighbour, thinking we have more knowledge or wisdom, a deeper understanding of the truth. We should be grateful for what we have and always seek to learn more. We are enjoined to love our neighbour, and that means we wish the best for him. Our Lord said to his disciples, "I am among you as one who serves." Do we need any other example?

Many people live largely on the physical plane. The body is all-important and its needs and desires must be met, so we work to earn money to buy food and shelter and all the various comforts we hanker after.

Others live partly on the physical and partly on the mental plane, and amongst these are the thinkers, writers, artists, inventors, etc.—people who ask questions and seek answers. These usually live a fuller and more satisfying existence, feeling in most cases that there is something meaningful to live for.

Still others live on all three planes. They know that life goes beyond the fourth dimension; they know that life is "more than meat, and the body than raiment." They live in the firm knowledge that God loves them and that whatever happens, He is ultimately in control. This can result in an inner peace and trust that is unshakeable in spite of outer circumstances. This inner peace has a calming and strengthening effect on both mind and body and assists enormously in maintaining and regaining health.

On the other hand, an unhealthy body and/or mind can have a weakening effect on the spiritual life. To achieve true health one needs total health—health of body, mind, and spirit. To achieve spiritual health our spirits need to be invaded by the spirit of God and to be "taken over"; this involves a complete surrender on our part and a continual daily surrender to God's will. And as time goes on and years pass, we will learn more of our complex selves—our weaknesses, our failings, our downright wickedness—so that we can ask for help to give these up so that the Holy Spirit can take over these areas of our lives.

Six / What Is Disease?

It is easy to say that disease is the opposite of health or a temporary interruption of the healthy process. The orthodox view is that disease is due to the invasion of foreign organisms, such as parasites or bacteria, or foreign substances (including poisons). But think for a moment—in the case of an epidemic, say measles, some people will be very ill, some may die, others will have the disease mildly, and others escape it altogether. Why is this? If the invading bacteria are all equally virulent, and bacteriological evidence suggests they are, there must be some other factor present to explain the different reactions to the bacteria on the part of different sufferers.

At this point I must make a digression. A scientist named Sir Albert Howard was also working in India at about the same time as Sir Robert McCarrison. He was particularly interested in breeding healthy cattle and, working on similar lines to the Hunzas, added large amounts of compost to the soil, thus building up its fertility and health. Over the years his animals achieved such a high level of health and resistance to disease that even when they rubbed noses, across the boundary fence, with animals suffering from foot-and-mouth disease they never contracted it.

Let us start from a different angle—if you like, do some lateral thinking. Consider a group of people who have been brought up on a "healthy diet" as described in chapter 1. Like Sir Albert Howard's cattle, they should be and in fact are able to resist infection and remain healthy. Beyond these really healthy people there are all grades of states of health, according

32

to how much or little they have followed the rules of health. So health depends upon the state of the body, its balance, its inner cleanliness. People who are truly healthy rarely succumb to infection.

In my early twenties I used to get two or three colds a year and influenza every two or three years. In my late twenties, on the advice of my future wife, I adopted a "healthy" diet, and from then my health improved until the time came when I very occasionally had influenza and only rarely a cold.

I came to accept the Nature Cure view that colds and other acute infections, if treated properly, can do a lot of good in "cleansing" the system. In the case of an illness like influenza, the patient gets very hot, usually perspires freely, and may have diarrhoea. This suggests that the body is cleaning itself by increasing the elimination of waste materials, and this process can be assisted by fasting. Taking solid food or drugs of any kind will tend to stop or hold up the healing, and the influenza hangs on for up to two or even three weeks.

In January and February of 1933 I was working in Eastbourne during a fairly severe influenza outbreak. I saw something in the neighbourhood of seventy patients and persuaded them to fast for three days and then gradually build up on a good regime. All they were given was an innocuous bitter "medicine." They were all well at the end of a week, and the majority back at work. They all said they felt better than for a long time. Some said they felt "cleaner." There was one exception, a dentist, who insisted on taking several aspirin tablets daily—he developed otitis media, an abscess in the middle ear. It was some time before he returned to work.

The three partners I was working with also saw many influenza patients and treated them in the usual way at that time. A number of these patients developed complications such as pneumonia, and sadly, a few died. During this time I saw six or seven patients who had developed pneumonia before I saw them. They were treated on the same lines as I treated my earlier patients, and made good recoveries. One of them was a little girl of seven or eight who had Saint Vitus's dance (chorea); the fever burnt up the chorea, and after the pneumonia her health was normal.

This whole experience helped to convince me that disease is the result of wrong living—wrong diet, insufficient exercise, shock and/or injury, anxiety, stress, hatred, etc. These factors will create a condition of unhealth in body, mind, and spirit, and in this state the body and mind and spirit are liable to invasion, the body to bacteria, the mind to mental disturbances, and the spirit to evil thoughts and worse.

Now there can be a kind of cross-infection. For instance, Dr. MacKarnass and others have shown that in some cases mental illness (such as schizophrenia or manic-depressive illness) can be due to a food or drink allergy. A spiritual condition such as hate, resentment, or jealousy can help to bring on a physical illness such as arthritis.

Fever of almost any kind can be used to burn up the waste products in the system and eliminate them mainly by sweating, sometimes aided by diarrhoea, and occasionally by vomiting. Fever should never be suppressed; it may have to be controlled by tepid sponging, cold packs, or even a cold shower. If the fever is suppressed by overeating or by drugs the body will usually get back to seemingly normal health, but the patient does not feel well and has a period of convalescence lasting anything up to several weeks. On the other hand, the patient whose fever has been carefully monitored will feel very well, although a little weak, as soon as the high temperature has done its work. This weakness goes rapidly upon return to a healthy diet.

Seven / Human Relationships (Society)

From earliest times man has lived in groups, first the family group; later these became expanded into tribes. Still later, tribes joined together to become nations.

In the group there had to be harmony and loyalty because there was interdependence and dissention would lead to disruption. Each group was suspicious of other groups and they would contrive to keep apart, but as the population increased, this became more difficult and fighting took place when one group tried to extend its territory. Over the centuries this greed for land and other possessions continued on a larger scale up to the present day.

Now we have a world of many nations, a few superpowers, some moderately powerful, and many weak. Many of these distrust each other. The result is that each nation spends enormous sums of money to try to make itself safe. If only this colossal amount of money could be used to help the needy, improving our ability to meet the real needs of people—agriculture, forestry, water, communications, and health—we could make this world a paradise. The knowledge is there but not the will.

What is the answer to this appalling dilemma? Reconciliation. If only the national leaders would come together and be completely honest with each other, they would begin to understand each other's feelings and points of view. By coming to understand one another they would come to respect each other, and this is the beginning of love. Love can lead to reconciliation and forgiveness, and perfect love casts out fear. When love has cast out fear, the need for armaments has gone (except in a small way for controlling the criminal). As any sane person will admit, this is the most difficult thing for us to do, yet it is the only way to a peace that is not just the absence of war.

How can this come about? As a Christian, I believe there is only one way. Only when the spirit of God takes over and penetrates the personality can life be changed. God's own love and forgiveness can change us so that we begin to love and forgive others. This is reconciliation. This is the only way a sick society can be truly treated, and we should all be praying continually for this. There is a prayer for peace that can be used not only by Christians, but also by those of other faiths. It was used by Mahatma Gandhi and is used by many people today, including, I understand, Mother Theresa of Calcutta. It goes like this: "Lead me from death to life, from falsehood to truth. Lead me from despair to hope, from fear to trust, lead me from hate to love, from war to peace. Let peace fill our hearts, our world, our universe."

To build a whole and healthy society the individuals, or at least the great majority, must be whole, so we each have an individual responsibility to this end. You cannot construct a strong building if most of your bricks are weak or damaged.

The Church should be the spearhead of the movement for health and holiness. When Jesus was on earth he healed and he taught, usually in that order. When he gave his disciples their instructions they were to teach and to heal and to baptise in his name—the threefold message for mind, body, and spirit. The Church consists of people who are being saved or healed.

Diseased bodies take time to heal; so many bodies are damaged and this damage takes time to repair, although in the all too rare case this healing can be rapid or even instantaneous when the immense healing power of the spirit activates the innate healing powers of the individual.

Diseased minds take time to heal, but again, the power of love (and God is love) can and does heal both mind and spirit. Before this healing can take place there has to be repentance. To repent is not merely to be sorry but infers a determination to turn from one's wrong ways and take a better way. This can involve changing one's diet, giving up harmful habits—tobacco, alcohol and other drugs, misuse of sex, lack of exercise, etc. For the serious Christian this involves a deeper surrender or commitment to God's will.

The Church is sick—it is divided. Our Lord prayed, in John's Gospel, chapter 17, that we should all be one. It is our great sin that we are not. How can we become one and fulfill Our Lord's greatest wish? What are the reasons for the many splits in the Church? I would humbly suggest they are mainly two—dogma and lack of love.

Love is God-given; dogma is man-made. The early Church had one simple dogma—Jesus is Lord. Paul states it clearly: "If thou shalt believe in thy heart and confess with thy mouth that Jesus is Lord, thou shalt be saved." From that one tremendous fact everything else follows. It seems to me tragic that we have to argue points of doctrine and practice as though they were essential, when we could be missing the life and health that Jesus the Lord is longing to bring to us. It reminds me of the man in Bunyan's *Pilgrim's Progress,* so intent on pursuit of treasure that he cannot see the Crown of Life being held out to him to take freely.

Our Lord gave his disciples very few commands. The first was: "Follow me." A challenge indeed, and one that I so often fail to reach. Another time he said, "A new commandment I give you, that you should love one another." Another tremendous challenge. As a young man I had very rigid views so that I could not conceive of my brother Christians holding different views. What do these differences matter? Truth is so immense and our minds so small that we can only grasp some small part of it. My brother may see another part (just like the five men and the elephant), but if we both agree that "Jesus is Lord," we can love one another. Love casts out fear; love unites. Dogma divides. That is not to say that we should do without dogma, but my dogma is my own interpretation of the truth and is for me alone, not to be impressed upon another.

How then can the Church be united? I believe that two things are certain. It will take time, and it will only be accomplished through the power of God's love. ("Not by might, not by power, but by My spirit saith the Lord.") True union cannot be imposed from above; it only tends to lead to further division, since some will remain outside. Unity is growing at the local level, where different churches and groups are joining together to pray, study, and worship together. I believe that only in this way will true union take place. There must be tolerance and understanding, which will grow into love. Only in this way shall we be following this further command of Our Lord that we should love one another. We can set up endless committees and discuss our differences—this may lead to better understanding, but will it lead to love? Only when we learn to pray and worship together will we come to love one another. When that happens our differences become unimportant, especially as we each come to realise that we can only feel "part of the elephant."

Another command Jesus gave us was to "do this in remembrance of me." It is one of the saddest things about the Church that there are such arguments centred around the Last Supper. The very number of names by which we call it expresses the different views about it—Eucharist, Holy Communion, the Lord's Supper, Breaking of Bread. Some branches of the Church do practise intercommunion. When all Christians of every denomination can and wish to join in a service of Communion together, that will constitute a deeper unity than any man-made act of union. Let us keep our different "forms" of worship; they suit different temperaments. For example, the Salvation Army services appeal to the outgoing, extroverted person, whilst the more introverted might prefer an Anglican Eucharist; the intellectual is often attracted to the Presbyterian or the Scottish kirk, the contemplative to the Friends, and so on.

Just before he left this earth, Jesus told his disciples, "Preach the gospel to all nations . . . and heal . . . " This, to me, infers that we should teach total healing, total salvation.

Eight / Pain and Suffering

Although the main theme of this book is health and healing, I think it would be incomplete without any reference to the subject of pain and suffering. I like to think of pain as physical and suffering as its mental counterpart. I wonder if remorse is pain on the spiritual level—it can be worse than physical pain, since it can shatter the ego. I speak as one who has experienced all three. Pain, suffering, and remorse are the direct result of man's sin. In the Kingdom of Heaven we are told there will be no more pain. But what can we do about pain now?

The first thing is to understand why there is pain. Pain is a warning that something is wrong. If we cut our finger or put our hand in something hot, we do something about it. If a leper who has lost all feeling in his hands cuts a finger or grasps something very hot, he feels no pain and may end up by cutting part of that finger right off or burning his hand severely. If we suffer pain in the chest, head, abdomen, etc., we try to find out the cause so that we can do something about it. In this, since pain is God-given, it is a signal that all is not well. Chronic pain, like chronic illness, e.g., arthritis, is the result of wrong living and also of suppressing acute illness such as colds and influenza.

Whatever happens, we should never blame God for "sending" pain to us. When, some time ago, I had shingles on the side of my head I had intense pain for six weeks, but I never blamed God. I kept thinking of His Son on that terrible Cross and thought, *Shingles cannot be remotely like the pain of*

40

crucifixion. The shingles was probably the result of a period of strain.

Pain and suffering are not necessarily or entirely our own fault. They can be the result of someone else's fault or the wrong of society as a whole. We can inherit deficiencies and can be injured through our own or another's fault. We are so bound up with one another, so interdependent, that we cannot singly reach full and complete health or perfection without the society in which we live growing together towards that perfection. So we owe it not only to ourselves, but also to our fellows to strive towards perfection, the salvation or health of body, mind, and spirit. Most of all, we owe it to God, Who initially endowed us with the will to strive for something better.

We have been given amazing bodies, wonderful minds, and even more wonderful spirits; we have been put into a world of immense power and remarkable beauty. Because we, mankind, have used all of these, which are, after all, only lent to us, selfishly and greedily we have brought pain and suffering into the world. If we will repent and follow God's laws, we can begin to reverse the current trend of destruction. Depend upon it; if we continue in our selfish, greedy, and grasping ways, we shall destroy this world and ourselves with it.

The choice is always the same in every generation, and that choice is ours—life or death.

Epilogue

Some who have managed to read this book to the end will say, "This is far too difficult; it sounds fine and it would be wonderful if we could all live together in health and harmony, but . . ." I would answer, "What is the alternative?" Either mankind has to grow up, physically, mentally, and spiritually, or we shall perish. We can deplete our resistance to ill health by living wrongly, poisoning the air, soil, and water, and fall victim to new disease; we can kill each other or blow ourselves up. Man has now such power available without the collective wisdom to use it for useful energy instead of destructive purposes.

I believe that God is calling us today to repent, to seek His will and follow it. Where we have sinned, i.e., come short of the Highest, we must make a firm decision to follow Him and to give up anything that hinders us from reaching the nearest to perfection possible. This could mean reforming one's diet, giving up tobacco and alcohol, refusing to read or watch salacious books and films, and learning to love and forgive instead of hate. All of these things, and more, can prevent the full surrender or commitment that Our Lord desires.

Too hard, is it? But Christ did not say it would be easy. He did say he would be with us always. And: "In the world you will have tribulation. But be of good cheer, I have overcome the world."

We live in a beautiful world that we are destroying, with ourselves, at an accelerating rate. We can halt and turn this process around. Have we the will to do it?

Postscript

In the last year or two since this book was completed, many things have been happening worldwide. There is an increasing appreciation of the fact that we are polluting and slowly destroying this planet. Trees are being felled at an increasing rate, and not being replaced, in South America, Central Africa, and the Far East. This will have a deleterious effect on the weather and also soil fertility and erosion. There is increasing concern about the ozone layer and the increase of gases, especially carbon dioxide, that have a deleterious effect on it. There is also increasing concern about pollution of our rivers, lakes, and shores from chemical effluents and sewage. There is also increasing concern about the purity and wholesomeness of our food.

All this concern is good, but are we tackling the problems fast enough and in the best way? The research of McCarrison and Howard shows that we have to begin with the soil—a healthy soil grows healthy plants, which, when consumed, produce healthy animals, including man. Furthermore, nothing should be regarded as waste. Everything can be recycled—metals, paper, glass, even sewage. Sewage should be composted with household waste, roadside sweepings, hedge cuttings, grass mowings, etc. Leaves should not be burnt but converted into rich leaf mould. Not long after the war, a system was invented in Denmark by which compost could be produced from sewage, household waste, etc., within a few days. This would obviate the pollution of our beaches and provide

43

an excellent and rich compost that could be sold to farmers and gardeners. Cans could be extracted by powerful electro-magnets and glass and other hardware screened off, the by-products then recycled.

There are other hopeful signs. Many of the nations are realising that cooperation is essential if we are to survive. The churches are drawing closer to each other and cooperating much more. Britain's own Prince of Wales is speaking out on these matters. One thing is certain: We need to change our attitude to life. Instead of going all out to make money, to seek a better "life-style," we should be devoting our lives to helping the less fortunate. Jesus summed it up in the words: "He that seeketh his life will lose it, he that loseth his life for my sake will find it."

Appendices

Appendix One

For those who want to reform their diet but are not sure how to begin, here is a suggested daily menu. Note: Preferably tea or coffee should be drunk at least one-half hour before a meal or an hour after.

Early morning. Tea (preferably weak China or Darjeeling)

Breakfast. Some kind of raw fruit (plenty of varieties to choose from)
Whole-meal cereal or muesli with milk or fruit juice
A little stewed fruit, e.g., prunes, apples, pears
If desired, whole-meal bread with butter or marmalade made with brown sugar (Demerara)

Midmorning. Tea (as above) or decaffeinated coffee or fruit juice

Lunch (interchangeable with supper). Meat, fish, or vegetarian dish (based on cheese, nuts, or legumes such as peas, beans, etc.)
Potatoes (excellent when baked in their jackets)
One or two other vegetables, preferably one green and the other root, onion, etc.
Stewed fruit with egg custard, junket, or rice (unpolished), etc., or any sweet made with whole-meal flour and fruit (fresh or dried)
Decaffeinated coffee

Tea. Tea (as above) or fruit juice

Supper (interchangeable with lunch). Egg, cheese, or nut
dish with green salad (at least three ingredients)
Whole-meal bread and butter
Honey or jam made with brown sugar (Demerara)
Raw fruit or fruitcake made with whole-meal flour

Most vegetarian cookery books give useful advice and
recipes. *Your Daily Bread,* by Doris Grant, is very useful and
helpful.

Homemade whole-meal bread is delicious and better than
anything you can buy.

Cook vegetables in very little water. Do not use pressure-
cooking.

You should not use salt, white sugar (including glucose),
white flour, or polished rice.

Malt vinegar is best avoided—use cider vinegar or lemon
juice in its place.

As stated earlier, I am against the use of alcoholic drinks—
in the long run they only do harm.

The less meat eaten, the better.

Always try to obtain organic whole-meal flour (100 percent). Health-food stores stock it when available.

Raw, untreated milk is much healthier than pasteurised,
sterilised, or "long-life" milk. The risk of infection is infinitesi-
mal. Raw milk contains beneficial bacteria that are destroyed
by heat. Raw milk turns sour on keeping—pasteurised milk
goes bad!

Appendix Two

I have not mentioned osteopathy, chiropractic, and manipulative medicine in the main body of the book since they belong more to the question of healing than to health itself, although one cannot, of course, have health without healing.

Practitioners who use manipulative methods are aware of the fact that slight deviations from the normal in the skeleton can produce various symptoms, the most common being pain. The pain is not necessarily at the site of the lesion but may be referred down a nerve such as the sciatic nerve (down the back of the thigh) or one of the intercostal nerves (running round the thorax just under the lower edge of each rib).

One of the most common pains, which is skeletal in origin, is lumbago or low back pain and its associate, sciatica. In over 90 percent of these cases, this is due to the sacroiliac joint becoming locked. This is a very important joint, since half of the weight of the trunk and the weight of the head and one arm is transmitted through it. Coming up from the ground, it is the first joint with movement in the vertical plane; it has a small range of movement (half an inch) and has very powerful, elastic ligaments to control this movement. Its main purpose is to act as a shock absorber, protecting the spine from jarring, e.g., when jumping off a chair. When one of the sacroiliac joints is locked or jammed, as the result of a fall or muscular effort, the whole area (muscles, etc.) goes into spasm, and this can be acutely painful. Pain can be transmitted along nerves to other parts of the body, such as the buttock, thigh, leg, foot, and lower part of the abdomen. When the joint is fully mobilised by suitable manipulative procedures, the pain and other symptoms clear up. This is just a general description, for this is not the place for a detailed thesis.

Many of the vertebral joints can become locked as the result of injury or sudden movement. The cervical vertebrae in the neck are particularly prone to this, and the trouble is readily diagnosed by a skilled manipulator. According to the level of the lesion, the patient may complain of headaches, pain in the neck, and/or pain in the shoulder, often travelling down the arm. Suitable manipulation corrects this. Lesions of the dorsal or thoracic vertebrae, i.e., the twelve vertebrae with ribs attached to them, can produce "girdle" pain, or pain in the front of the chest or abdomen. In some cases these lesions can have an influence on the working of the internal organs.

Peripheral joints, such as limb joints, are also subject to minor disorders following injury. Most people know of cartilage trouble in the knee joint when the cartilage becomes misplaced. It can be corrected by manipulation, provided the cartilage is intact (not torn or split). Sprained wrist and ankle joints respond well to manipulation. Cases of tennis elbow also usually respond well to manipulation.

This is a very brief description of how manipulative treatment, when appropriate, can help in the quest for better health.

Bibliography

Baker, Richard St. Barbe. *Green Glory.* London: Lutterworth Press, 1948.

————. *I Planted Trees.*

Carson, Rachel. *Silent Spring.* London: Penguin, 1962.

Cleave, Campbell, and Painter. *The Saccharin Disease.* New Canaan, Conn.: Keats Publishing, 1986.

Drummond, Henry. *The Greatest Thing in the World.* Boston: Branden Publishing, 1963.

Grant, Doris. *Your Daily Bread.* New Canaan, Conn.: Keats Publishing, 1974.

Hadfield, J. A. *Dreams and Nightmares.* London: Penguin Books, 1954.

Jenks, Jorian. *From the Ground Up.* London: Hollis & Carter. 1950.

Jung, Carl Gustav. *Memories, Dreams, and Reflexions.* Flamingo (Collins), 1983.

————. *Analytical Psychology.* London: Routledge and Kegan Paul, 1953.

Lawrence, Brother. *The Practice of the Presence of Christ.* London: Hodder, 1982.

McCarrison, Sir Robert. *Nutrition and Health.* London: McCarrison Society, circa 1935.

McKarness. *Not All in the Mind.* Pan, 1990.

Phillips, J.B. *New Testament Translated into Modern English.* London: Geoffrey Bles, 1957.

Rayner, Louise. *Trees and Toadstools.*

Weatherhead, Leslie. *Psychology, Religion and Healing.*